WORLDVIEW GUIDE

THE CANTERBURY TALES

Elizabeth Howard

canonpress
Moscow, Idaho

CONTENTS

INTRODUCTION

Spring has arrived, prompting folks from all stations of medieval life to pilgrimage together to the shrine of Thomas Becket. Because long trips tend to be rather dull, the travelers begin a storytelling competition featuring roosters, murders, bewitched hags, banished wives in barrels, plenty of adulterers, a whole host of churchmen, and a frying pan whisked to hell. Who will tell the best story on the way? That is for the host, Harry Bailey, to decide.

THE WORLD AROUND

In the decades between 1380 and 1400, the year Chaucer died, England was certainly reeling from a good deal of turmoil. Paramount was the devastation caused by the Black Death, which had just torn through England from 1348–1351, destroying a full third of her population.[1]

In addition to the social chaos, religious superstition, and grief that this plague caused, the loss of laborers to work the landed estates led to much political upheaval; the peasants now actually had the position to lobby for better treatment and better rights. They did just that in the Peasants' Revolt of 1381, challenging the rigidity of the feudal structure.[2]

Alongside the Peasants' Revolt against the nobility, complaints against the abuses of the Catholic Church

---

1. John Hatcher, "England in the Aftermath of the Black Death," *Past & Present* 144 (1994): 3.
2. Ibid., 27.

were quickly multiplying. The Protestant Reformation was about to break on the horizon of medieval England. While John Wycliffe is, perhaps, the most well-known English spokesman against abuses in the church at this time, the Lollards, who referenced large portions of Wycliffe's teaching, were the most vocal in broadcasting these abuses. Between rumblings in the culture at large and among some of his own friends, Chaucer was not far removed from the growing complaints against the church.

Additionally, William the Conqueror's invasion of England with the hordes of French-speaking nobility whom he brought along propelled the English language through a Great Vowel Shift; the language had grown up out of Anglo-Saxon Old English to Middle English with its sweet, romantic vowel sounds. Middle English became a literary language—one robust enough to sustain dramatic poetry—with the publication of Chaucer's *Canterbury Tales* and his *Troilus and Criseyde*.

ABOUT THE AUTHOR

Geoffrey Chaucer was not a reclusive, scholarly poet. Rather than spending most of his time scribbling and composing in his private study, Chaucer spent most of his career in a highly public and political role.

Chaucer primarily worked for Edward III and Richard II as an ambassador (and spy) on the European continent. In this capacity, he traveled extensively, spending time in France (1360), Spain (1366), and Italy (1372–1373). In his travels he encountered various, contemporary literary geniuses such as Boccaccio and Petrarch.[3] Truth be told, Chaucer actually borrowed a good handful of plot lines for the stories of *The Canterbury Tales* from authors like Boccaccio and Petrarch. In fact the very structure of *The Canterbury Tales* mimics Boccaccio's *Decameron*. It would

---

3. Geoffrey Chaucer, *The Canterbury Tales,* ed. Walter Skeat (Oxford: Clarendon Press, 1906), 31.

be nearly impossible to overestimate the influence of Chaucer's travels and those he met on his own work.

Because of his courtly responsibilities, Chaucer developed into a proficient translator—not only of official royal documents, but also of literary works. He is known for his translations of *The Romance of the Rose* from French and *The Consolation of Philosophy* from Latin. His facility with a number of languages also exposed him to a variety of genres of literature outside of the English canon. Consequently, Chaucer learned to compose in a wide range of genres: courtly romances, dream visions, frame narratives, ballads, fables, and poetry. This literary breadth was necessary for an author who would compose more than two dozen different tales in the mouths of a troop of characters journeying to Canterbury.

WHAT OTHER
NOTABLES SAID

While C.S. Lewis did appreciate Chaucer's work, he was initially unimpressed with the majority of *The Canterbury Tales*. In a letter to his friend Arthur Greeves, he remarks, "I have now read all the Tales of Chaucer […] Some of them are quite impossible. On the whole, with one or two exceptions, like the Knight's Tale and the Franklin's, he is disappointing when you get to know him. He has most of the faults of the Middle Ages—garrulity and coarseness—without their romantic charm."[4]

Those, meanwhile, who admire Chaucer's *Canterbury Tales* largely fall into two camps: some critics celebrate

4. Walter Hooper, ed., *The Collected Letters of C.S. Lewis*, vol. 1, *Family Letters 1905-1931*, [Letter to Arthur Greeves, June 14, 1916] 192. He later retracted his opinion and praised the tales as "glorious reading," albeit not influential on medieval poetry. See *The Allegory of Love: A Study in Medieval Tradition* (New York: Oxford University Press, 1958), 203.

the way Chaucer shaped a crude form of Middle English into a poetic language, both serious and playful, while others marvel at the sheer range of characters and tales he brought to life.

Harold Bloom praises Chaucer's linguistic achievement: "Together with Shakespeare and a handful of the greater novelists in English, Chaucer carries the language further into unthinkable triumphs of representations of reality than ought to be possible."[5]

Similarly, the translator for our version of *Canterbury Tales*, John Urban Nicolson, describes his admiration for Chaucer's original poetry this way: "My unwavering desire has been to offer [in modern translation] that which may prove provocative of further interest upon the part of the reader. With this apology, I set forth a diluted drink. May it arouse an enduring thirst for the older and more potent liquor."[6]

Eighteen-century poet John Dryden argues, meanwhile, that Chaucer's genius lies in the scope of his imagination: "[Chaucer] must have been a Man of a most wonderful comprehensive Nature. [...] [H]e has taken into the Compass of his *Canterbury Tales* the various Manners and Humors [...] of the whole English Nation, in his Age. [...] All his pilgrims are severally distinguish'd from each

---

5. Harold Bloom, ed., "Introduction," in *Modern Critical Views Geoffrey Chaucer* (New York: Chelsea House Publishers, 1985), 1.

6. All quotations taken from Nicolson's translation (Garden City, New York: Garden City Publishing, 1934), xi-xii.

other. […] 'Tis sufficient to say, according to the Proverb, that here is God's Plenty."[7]

G.K. Chesterton similarly praises Chaucer: "The Poet is the Maker; he is the creator of a cosmos; and Chaucer is the creator of the whole world of his creatures. He made the pilgrimage; he made the pilgrims."[8] Chesterton goes so far as to make Chaucer's parading cast the predecessor to the novel genre: "[Chaucer] is not only the father of all our poets, but the grandfather of all our hundred million novelists. It is rather a responsibility for him."[9]

---

7. John Dryden, "Preface," in *Fables Ancient and Modern* (London: J. Tonson, 1721), https://babel.hathitrust.org/cgi/pt?id=nnc1.0022477705;view=1up;seq=29.

8. Chesterton, "The Greatness of Chaucer," in *Chaucer* (London: Faber and Faber, 1932), 21.

9. Ibid.

SETTING, CHARACTERS
AND PLOT SUMMARY

- *Setting: The story begins at the Tabard Inn, but the tales are narrated on route to the shrine of St. Thomas Becket in Canterbury.*
- *Narrator:* Believed by most to be Chaucer himself, though he remains unnamed in the text.
- *Harry Bailey:* The host of the pilgrim party at the Tabard Inn who volunteers to travel with the pilgrims on their way and initiates the storytelling competition.
- *The Clerk:* A poor scholar who devotes all of his money to books.
- *The Prioress:* A nun named Madame Eglantine who appears all proper and holy, but speaks French with a feigned accent and seems to care very little for those in actual poverty and suffering.

- *The Nun's Priest:* Not much is said of him in the prologue, but he accompanies the Prioress as her confessor as they travel.
- *The Friar:* A rotund, merry churchman named Hubert who has a license to travel around preaching and asking for alms—a privilege he is taking advantage of, given his girth, familiarity with young women, and fancy clothing.
- *The Summoner:* The friar's rival in storytelling who is as hot-headed as the friar is merry. He is supposed to bring debtors and law-breakers to court for trial, but he makes most of his living, leveling false accusations and demanding bribes to drop charges.
- *The Knight:* A crusader recently returned from the Holy Land, one of two nobles in the pilgrim company.
- *The Lawyer:* He is a wealthy fellow who charges much for his legal cases but doesn't really seem to get much work done.
- *The Wife of Bath:* Alison is larger than life. She dresses flamboyantly, has been married five times (not to mention other lovers), and has become a self-proclaimed expert on romantic relationships. On the side, she makes and sells cloth.
- *The Pardoner:* A stringy-haired churchman whose job it is to hear confession and pardon

sins. He travels around with a bag of fake relics
that he deceives folks into paying money to see.

- *The Parson:* One of two men whom the narra-
tor describes as good and kind. He takes care
of his congregation's needs and teaches them
faithfully.

- *The Plowman:* The other favorite of the narrator
and the brother of the Parson. He is a man of
the land who works hard for his bread and loves
God and his neighbor.

From a narrative standpoint, the basic storyline of *The
Canterbury Tales* covers little more than what the title
suggests: a group of pilgrims travel together to Canter-
bury and compete, at the encouragement of the host, with
one another to tell tales on the way. We call *Canterbury*
a "frame narrative" because the story of the pilgrims and
their storytelling is the larger story inside of which Chau-
cer is able to narrate all of his other tales. He uses the
mouths of his imaginary pilgrims as the vehicles to tell
a vast array of stories in many genres including the fa-
ble, the saint's life, the classical romance, the sermon, and
the *fabliau* (the cousin to the fable, without the moral at
the end). Once the pilgrims begin to tell their tales, they
only speak directly to one another in the prologues to the
tales, where the host often has to resolve arguments, si-
lence bossy travelers, or draw the reserved ones into the
competition.

Given the instructions of the host in the "General Prologue," Chaucer apparently planned to pen 120 tales, since each of the thirty pilgrims were instructed to tell two tales on the way to Canterbury and two more on the way home. *Canterbury Tales* is, therefore, considered an incomplete work since Chaucer was only able to finish twenty-four tales between 1380 and his death.

While the tales range widely from the dry and tedious or instructive to the scandalous and obscene or the absurd and humorous, each tale pairs uniquely with its narrator. Each tale becomes a sort of commentary on each pilgrim narrator; the fact that the Miller and the Reeve tell such bawdy tales reveals much about their characters. Similarly the introduction of the pilgrims in the "General Prologue" prepares the reader for the tales that follow.

The breadth of the tales showcases the literary craftsmanship of Chaucer, but few, if any, of the tales originated with Chaucer; he borrowed the storylines for most tales from ancient texts, the popular stories in England and across the continent, and sometimes from the published works of his contemporaries. Before condemning Chaucer for plagiarism, however, it is important to keep in mind that the medieval act of reading was one of rewriting: the act of imitation and adaption was a great sign of respect and admiration—as well as a way for Chaucer to show off. The logic is fairly simple: if Chaucer can write Petrarch's stories better than Petrarch, what a very splendid author Chaucer proves himself to be.

WORLDVIEW ANALYSIS

Chaucer's *Canterbury Tales* seem structurally simple: a long train of stories told by a range of pilgrims. The connections between the tales, however, feel far more elusive. Even Boccaccio, Chaucer's Italian literary contemporary brought the worldview of his own frame narrative more easily to the surface. Boccaccio sets his *Decameron* in the middle of the Black Death's rapid spread throughout the Italian peninsula. The ten companions decide to escape from the plague to the countryside and spend their days with nothing better to do but "eat, drink, and be merry"—telling tales to pass the time while they wait for the plague to pass over or to infect them too. For Boccaccio, stories are the best antidotes to disease as they offer diversion while putting the present tragic circumstances in the larger context of the human drama. For Chaucer, however, the narrative plot thread seems no stronger than a smattering of spontaneous vignettes motivated by competition and boredom on the road.

The breath of the characters also complicates the teasing out of Chaucer's worldview; Chaucer can hide himself by speaking in so many voices and from many vantages. Can such a frame narrative have any sort of worldview integrity, or must such a work's worldview be simply defined as the aggregate of the thirty travelers' worldviews?

Some critics have argued that Chaucer's goal was merely to give us a survey of "all walks of life" in Medieval England in the late 1300s. From the list of pilgrims, we see the Knight and his son, the Squire, representing the landed class. Chaucer also gives us a long list of churchmen and women including the Friar, the Monk, the Prioress, the Nun's Priest, the Summoner, the Pardoner, and the Parson, as well as a gaggle of lay folk and laborers like the Miller, the Reeve, and the Plowman, among many others. These three social groupings give us the three estates common to Medieval England. Some have suggested that rather than merely present how the three estates interacted in his day and age, Chaucer sought to comment upon the social setup of Medieval England by creating an "estate satire," one that mocked certain absurdities in all classes by having members of each estate tell tales responding to others from other classes. Chaucer also introduces members that don't fit nicely into the three estates—members of what appears to be the future middle class: the Man of Law, the Merchant, the land-owning Franklin, and perhaps the Wife of Bath. And indeed much of the story holds together as a string of interactions between characters moderated by the host. For example, the Friar responds to the Wife of Bath, the Summoner responds to the Friar, the Clerk responds to the Wife of Bath, and so on and so forth.

The action of "narration and counter-narration or a response narrator" between Pilgrims is indeed strong throughout the tales, even if the responses aren't always between estates (oftentimes, the competition is between members of the same social class like the Miller and the Reeve or the Friar and the Summoner). We call this urge among the pilgrims to respond one to another, either with a better story or with an attack on the previous narrator, "*quitting*," and Chaucer's characters model it in one of two ways. If it is done in good humor between two characters, we call the response tale one of *game* (pronounced *gā-me*).[10] If it is done in a serious spirit, either to instruct morally or to harm the previous narrator, we call the response tale one of *entente* (pronounced like our modern English word *intent*).[11]

Chaucer lends the reader much help in determining which stories are those of *game* and which are those of *entente* with the different poetic forms he employs in the

---

10. *Middle English Dictionary*, s.v. "Gāme," Middle English Dictionary, University of Michigan, http://quod.lib.umich.edu/cgi/m/mec/med-idx?type=id&id=MED18146 (accessed Dec. 7, 2016).
11. Ibid., s.v. "Entente."

Middle English. For stories and interactions of *game*, Chaucer writes in rhyming couplets or two-line stanzas. When the tale is serious in theme or when Chaucer wishes to communicate a more serious tone, he has his character narrate in rhyme royal. Rhyme royal is a poetic stanza created by Chaucer with seven lines that follow the rhyme scheme *a b a b b c c*. The Rhyme Royal stanza has two couplets at the end but that first couplet is interwoven poetically with the first three lines (or tercet). Such poetic "keys" or markers help the reader trace Chaucer's own intentions in crafting particular characters and stories.

In tracing Chaucer's worldview and that of his cast of characters, we must remember, in response to those who argue that Chaucer simply meant to display Medieval life in the late 1300s or that he simply meant to satirize the three estates, that Chaucer did indeed craft or invent these characters. Chaucer certainly disguises his voice as that of the narrator in the text who is merely "recounting" or "relaying" what he has heard on the road, but Chesterton reminds us that Chaucer is principally a creator or maker, fashioning each member of the troop and placing him or her in a web of relationships that he likewise arranges and directs.

So what might Chaucer seek to accomplish with the particular band gathered at the Tabard Inn besides competing in his narrative gamesmanship with the contemporary authors of his day? Organizing the characters into descriptions that are critical, ambivalent, or favorable offers at least one schema for analyzing them in relation to Chaucer's worldview. Some characters Chaucer seems openly hostile towards. For example, he describes the Summoner's face as full of pimples and red enough to scare little children and then describes the Summoner's actions as those of a liar, an extorter, and a crook.

For the majority of the troop, however, Chaucer is a bit more subtle with his opinion, allowing the reader to judge the characters more accurately themselves from the evidence he provides. What ought we to make of a friar who, instead of observing his vows of poverty dictated by the Rule of his mendicant order, gives the biggest and best absolutions to those who give him the greatest alms? He is portly fellow, a frequent visitor to taverns, and one arrayed in fine cloaks. Yes, Chaucer is critical of the Friar, but his criticism decries the inconsistency between the behavior one might expect from a holy father and the persona of jolly Hubert. Similarly the Prioress seems pious and dainty as befits a head matron in a nunnery. She, however, tells a bloody tale of communal violence committed by the Jewish community. Chaucer also introduces her with a bizarre argument of silence. He tells us that she feeds tasty bread to the little dogs under the table, but she shows no evidence of performing true acts of charity. When the Syrophoenican woman tells Jesus in the gospels, "Even the little dogs get the scraps under the table," she is asking Jesus to help her, not to feed little dogs. The Prioress, however, privileges the dogs, mistaking the priorities of her order. In the same way, we expect the Monk to be dedicated to the study and preaching of God's word, but he prefers hunting and traveling. The Pardoner tells a tale in which he exhorts men to repent of their sins, but he then swindles them out of their money by demanding pay to kiss his false relics for their forgiveness. Is this the sort of Pardoner we would want in our parish? Notice that of the three estates, Chaucer is suspicious of almost all of those connected with the church.

Other pilgrims act as we might expect: the Knight finds his inspiration in the classics. He is duty-bound like the heroes of old. His son, meanwhile, is handsome and vain. The Wife of Bath, who has wed five husbands, is spunky and unconventional. The Clerk acts like a modern honors student: he is poor and busy, spending all of his money on books and all of his time reading them. Chaucer has little to say against such characters but little to say in praise of them.

There are two notable exceptions: the Parson and the Plowman. Chaucer openly praises these two. After the long list of swindling, greedy, frivolous churchmen, Chaucer introduces a parson who practices what he preaches and models godliness for his small parish. He stewards his position with faithfulness. Finally, in his tale, the Parson gives a very long, expository sermon on charity (while the Friar completely bungles the sermon form in his own tale). That Chaucer praises the Parson's behavior and demeanor so strongly may illuminate Chaucer's own complaints against Medieval England: in a crowd of churchmen, there are but few who do their work without corruption. Such a depiction begs for reformation in this cast of pilgrims and throughout the country.

Remembering that Chaucer writes just before the dawn of the English reformation also helps us understand his praise of the Plowman. Less than a decade before Chaucer began composing *The Canterbury Tales*, William Langland, a more vocal dissenter against the abuses in the Catholic Church at the time, wrote a popular dream vision poem called *Pier's Plowman* in which he praised the honest, hardworking layfolk of England who did their work honestly and faithfully and were, in turn, rewarded by God. Chaucer's Plowman is such a man; he puts others before himself and works diligently day-in and day-out in the fields.

Now, if it is true that Chaucer is indeed joining, at least from a distance, those decrying the abuses of the church in his critique of so many churchmen and his praise of the faithful layman and local parson, we must note the care with which he does so. Chaucer's friend, John Gower wrote openly attacking the church (as well as corruptions in the other two estates) in *Vox Clamantis* and *Mirour de l'Omme*.[12] *Vox Clamantis* is the way John the Baptist refers

---

12. For selections from Gower's *Vox Clamantis* and *Mirour de l'Omme*, see Norton Topics Online, "Medieval Estates and Orders—Making

to himself: "the voice of one crying in the wilderness." And the second title suggests that Gower wishes to hold a mirror up to man so that he can rightly see himself. Such bold rhetorical moves were dangerous in the fourteenth century, and we must remember that Chaucer was working for the royal courts of both Richard II and Edward III.

Safer even than the plausible deniability offered by the excuse of Langland's dream vision: "I am just recording a dream I had," Chaucer's frame narrative allows him to distance himself from any direct accusation of the church. He is merely recounting a group of travelers he has met and the stories they have chosen to tell

Nonetheless, the concern over the immorality and corruption is evident: there are so few tales told like that of Griselda and so many told of bawds, trickery, and blasphemy. As readers we cannot but be discouraged that the imaginations of so many pilgrims headed to a holy site on a holy pilgrimage are full of so many distractions. We might aptly compare the situation to a long string of bathroom jokes and inappropriate racist and sexist stories recounted at length by a church youth group en route to a month-long missions trip, all goaded on by the youth pastor himself.

And so Chaucer gives us Medieval England and a picture of human nature in all its diverse forms, but he

---

and Breaking Rules," The Norton Anthology of English Literature, accessed on December 7, 2016, http://www.wwnorton.com/college/english/nael/middleages/topic_1/satire.htm.

does not do so ambivalently. He is not merely a passive bystander to the rough humor and the pointed attacks. Amidst the enthusiastic story competition, he shows us what fools these travelers can be: clever in their own eyes but condemned by their words and actions. Thus Chaucer leaves his readers with the longing that we might find more folk like the Parson and the Plowman on the road to Canterbury.

QUOTABLES

1. "When April with his showers sweet with fruit
   The drought of March has pierced unto the root
   And bathed each vein with liquor that has power
   To generate therein and sire the flower; […]
   (So Nature pricks them on to ramp and rage) —
   Then do folk long to go on pilgrimage,
   And palmers to go seeking out strange strands,
   To distant shrines well known in sundry lands.
   And specially from every shire's end
   Of England they to Canterbury wend,
   The holy blessed martyr there to seek
   Who helped them when they lay so ill and weak."[13]
                                        —Narrator

2. "And therefore, pretty Pertelote, my dear,
   By such old-time examples may you hear
   And learn that no man should be too reckless

---

13. Nicolson, 1.

Of dreams, for I can tell you, fair mistress,
That many a dream is something well to dread."[14]

—Chanticleer

3. "Well, sometimes we are God's own instruments
    And means to do His orders and intents,
    When so He pleases, upon all creatures,
    In divers ways and shapes, and divers features.
    Without Him we've no power, 'tis certain,
    If He be pleased to stand against our train."[15]

—The Devil

4. "With him there was a plowman, was his brother,
    That many a load of dung, and many another
    Had scattered, for a good true toiler, he,
    Living in peace and perfect charity.
    He loved God most, and that with his whole heart
    At all time, though he played or plied his art,
    And next, his neighbor, even as himself.
    He'd thresh and dig, with never thought of pelf."[16]

—Said of the Plowman

---

14. Nicolson, 273.

15. Ibid., 351.

16. Ibid.

21 SIGNIFICANT
QUESTIONS AND ANSWERS

1. What impression do you get from the narrator's description of the pilgrims? How might we characterize the crowd?

> The narrator notices a lot of details about the pilgrims, and he seems to know an awful lot about them for just having met them at the Tabard Inn. There seem to be a broad range of characters: lots of different classes, including nobility, the churchmen, and the poor. There seems to be a broad range of personalities and standards of morality. This might suggest that Chaucer is showing us the interactions of "all walks of life" which is difficult to find in medieval life outside of the pilgrimage road.

2. Do any descriptions seem out of place for the char-
    acters described? How do the characters' descriptions
    match the tales they tell?

    > Answers may vary but characters like the Friar
    > seem perhaps too chubby to be a monastic ascetic.
    > Furthermore, the comment that he loves giving gifts
    > of knives to young wives and the fact that he is aw-
    > fully good at marrying off young women seems more
    > than a bit out of place for a man who is to devote his
    > life to caring for the poor and preaching. He ought
    > to forgive those who come to him confessing, but
    > it seems as if he is most quick to forgive those who
    > pay the highest price.[17] Similarly, the Prioress can't
    > stand the sight of a mouse harmed in a trap and gives
    > the "fine white bread"[18] to the dogs under the table,
    > but that seems awfully suspicious for a woman who
    > should be feeding the poor. Why is she giving such
    > bread to the dogs?

3. What sorts of motives ought to drive pilgrims to
    journey to Thomas Becket's shrine? From the text of
    the "Opening Prologue," what seems to motivate this
    company?

    > The narrator suggests that pilgrims usually head
    > to the shrine of Thomas Becket to thank him for
    > healing them when they had all "lay so ill and weak"
    > throughout the winter months.[19] Pilgrimages were

---

17. Nicolson, 7-8.

18. Ibid., 5.

19. Ibid., 1.

a religious act of thanks. Nevertheless, like the diversity of the crowd, the motives of the travelers also seem to range widely. The Wife of Bath and the Knight have both traveled on pilgrimages before, but the Wife of Bath seems more interested in sharing "remedies of love"[20] than any spiritual exhortations. The Knight, meanwhile, seems to see his pilgrimage as part and parcel with his fighting in the Holy Lands. He has just returned home from Palestine and immediately sets off for Canterbury, suggesting either that he loves travel or considers such pilgrimages his duty.[21] Meanwhile the monk hates being locked up in a cell in study, so he heads out in search of diversion and adventuring.[22]

4. Given the way the storytelling game is set up by the host, what might be some of the challenges that could complicate its successful completion?

Beyond the simple fact that telling 120 stories is a massive undertaking for the pilgrims to tell and the narrator to record, the host leaves it a bit unclear who will judge the competition at the end. It seems that he might have some significant power in deciding the victor since he initiated the game and the winner will be declared back at his inn.[23] Meanwhile, it is our narrator who actually tells us the tales, and we must trust his narration of them.

---

20. Ibid., 15.
21. Ibid., 3.
22. Ibid., 7.
23. Ibid., 24.

We have a competition about storytelling in which
one narrator relates all of the tales that are told.
Who is the master storyteller then? The narrator?

5.   What is the basic plot of "The Nun's Priest's Tale"?

A rooster and hen husband and wife debate
the validity of prophetic dreams. The haughty
Chanticleer dreams he will be eaten by a fox, and
his wife scoffs at his fears. They debate the legiti-
macy of dreams at length. Eventually Chanticleer
carries on with his haughty strutting in the hen
house, but becomes more insufferable, making his
wives bring him his meals as he is afraid to walk
outside at all lest the fox catch him. In the end, the
fox does catch the tasty fowl, but Chanticleer ap-
peals to the fox's own vanity and tricks the fox into
opening his mouth, and thus the flatterer escapes
to strut another day.

6.   Examine the poetic form of "The Nun's Priest's Tale."
What does this tell us about the genre of the tale?

It is written in rhyming couplets and not rhyme
royal so it does not bear the same moral weight
and seriousness that "The Clerk's Tale" bears, for
example.

7. Compare the husband that the widow has had with Pertelote's husband Chanticleer.

> The widow's husband had provided for her financially even in her widowhood. Meanwhile Chanticleer is so fearful for his own safety that he makes his many wives pick up grain for him. His wife shuns him, "Now have you lost my heart and all my love I cannot love a coward, by my faith".[24]

8. How many narrative layers do we have in the tale that Chanticleer tells Pertelote? What might Chaucer be doing here?

> The narrator is retelling "The Nun's Priest's Tale" about a rooster. At this point the rooster is telling a story about the foreshadowing dream of the murdered man or of Saint Kenelm, so we have a story within a story within a story. Chaucer can show off by narrating yet another story set inside the common Fable of Chanticleer and Pertelote. Chanticleer also seems to be establishing his authority as he lists both biblical and historical examples of those whose dreams were true warnings.

9. According to Nun's Priest, who is to blame for Chanticleer's death? Was the dream a necessary end for Chanticleer, or a possible end?

> It seems as if the Nun's Priest treats the tragedy of Chanticleer as a tragedy of necessity, one in which

24. Nicolson, 267.

Chanticleer has no possibility of escape. See in particular lines like "You were well warned, and fully, by your dreams / That this day should hold peril damnably. / But that which God foreknows, it needs must be."[25] The Nun's Priest also cries "O destiny, you cannot be eschewed".[26] Nevertheless, the Nun's Priest acknowledges that he doesn't actually want to present a full reading on God's foreknowing and human freedom.[27] The Nun's Priest also explores woman as the possible guilty party since it is Pertelote who encourages her husband not to listen to the dream, but he also refuses to hold this position dogmatically.[28] As it works out in the tale, it seems that it is Chanticleer's own pride and haughtiness that get him caught by the fox.

10. What do we make of the ending of "The Nun's Priest's Tale" with Chanticleer's escape?

This fable obviously lacks any poetic justice since the haughty, fearful cock gets away with his temerity and pride. Nonetheless, the Nun's Priest is still able to use the story to issue his warning not to be "indiscreet in governance".[29]

---

25. Ibid., 275.
26. Nicolson, 278.
27. Ibid., 276.
28. Ibid.
29. Ibid., 281.

11. What is the plot of "The Pardoner's Tale"?

> "The Pardoner's Tale" also warns against pre-
> sumption when three profane drunkards hear
> news that Death lives near by, guarding a pile of
> gold. Dismissive of the warnings surrounding the
> treasure, the men seek out the treasure. Greed
> overpowers each of them as they figure out how to
> procure provisions without leaving the gold. Two
> guard the treasure while the third goes into town to
> buy food and drink. The two guardians conspire to
> kill their companion as soon as he returns so they
> only need to split the treasure between themselves.
> Meanwhile, the man sent to town poisons the
> provisions so that he will have the treasure all to
> himself. Thus Death catches all three men.

12. How does the Pardoner's direct attack on drunken-
ness and gluttony at the story's beginning change our
dispositions towards the main characters? How is this
different from the tale of Chanticleer?

> While we are tempted to cheer for Chanticleer and
> to hope for his survival, the Pardoner sets us up to
> despise the roisterers from the beginning. This is
> very ironic considering the fact that the Pardoner is
> intentionally cheating those he pardons with fake
> relics that are actually just pig bones.

13. What connection might we make between Death's lair and the mound of gold under the tree located in the same place? What might the Pardoner be suggesting?

> Rather than blaming Death as the ultimate foe, the Pardoner seems to shift the blame for murders off of personified death and onto the greed, gluttony, and wickedness of men. Yes, Death kills many, the Pardoner seems to argue, but men are his main agents, even if unwittingly.

14. How is the Pardoner's tale a better example of poetic justice than the Nun's Priest's tale?

> The three greedy roisterers all end up dead while they have attempted to murder their companions. They seem to bring judgment on their own heads in their attempt to satisfy their own greed. Meanwhile, in "The Nun's Priest's Tale," Chanticleer evades the Fox in the end despite his obvious fault of pride and self-assurance.

15. How does the Pardoner's "sales pitch" for absolution and forgiveness color the dramatic tale he tells on the danger of committing grievous sins?

> Instead of receiving the Pardoner's tale as the genuine concern from a churchman for the souls of his people like the Parson's sermon, the Pardoner ultimately seems only interested in pricking the consciences of his audience in order to get them

to pay him. In many ways, he is as crooked as the
roisterers whose tale he tells.

16. What is the Friar trying to do with his tale?

The Friar uses his tale to goad on the journeying
Summoner and expose his greed by crafting a story
about a wicked Summoner who partners with the
Devil for the day to see what they can collect from
those they meet.

17. What is the basic plot of the Friar's Tale?

While the Devil acts as a perfect gentleman, only
taking things freely offered to him, the Summoner
tries to foist false charges on an old widow and so
extort her out of her last earnings. When she insists,
"The Devil take you," off goes the Summoner to
hell along with the frying pan, which she also curs-
es. The original moral to the tale warned the reader
to be careful with swearing and foreswearing. The
friar, however, emends the moral to warn everyone
everywhere about summoners, whom, he concludes,
are just a bad lot.

18. Notice the poetic form of the Friar's tale. What does
that tell us about the tale? Does the tale effectively
warn us against swearing?

"The Friar's Tale" is also told in rhyming cou-
plets, so it is a story of *game* instead of *entente* (a
light-hearted tale rather than a morally serious

one). Nonetheless the Summoner seems to take it quite seriously and is extremely offended when the friar makes him the object of damnation. It is worth asking if a friar ought to joke about theologically serious matters like condemning another to hell. The very point of the story he tells suggests that one should not joke about such matters because swearing might cause the devil to take a soul to hell. And yet, despite his clear narrative moral against frivolous swearing and joking about damnation, the friar commits the very error he warns against.

19. Consider the presentation of the devil in the tale: Is he really that devilish? What would a devilish devil look like?

The devil seems a sort of gentlemen in the Friar's tale. He is patient to ensure that things sworn over to him are done so with full intention, unlike the Summoner who wishes to extort and steal. In fact, the devil appears more like the Friar: he is merry and jovial. He is a pleasant companion for the Summoner on his rounds. Although the Friar warns that the devil is a dangerous foe, he doesn't seem to present him as such. Rather, it seems like the Friar is more concerned with presenting summoners as dangerous foes.

20. What theology of evil does the Friar give us when his devil announces that devils are "God's own instruments"?[30]

> The Friar seems rather orthodox here, arguing that even demons must service the purposes of God in the same way that Joseph explains to his brothers in the book of Genesis that what they intended for evil God intended for good. The Friar notes ironically that devils might actually lead a man to salvation when they tempt him, and he, in response, flees to Christ. A contemporary of Chaucer, John Felton, plays with this very theme in a short illustration he gave for a sermon on Psalm 32:1, "Blessed are they whose iniquities are forgiven; whose sins are covered": "There was a demonic who told many what kind of people they were. To one he said, 'You are such and such a man' and told him many sins. The man left at once, confessed, and then asked the demoniac, 'What do you say about me?' And the demoniac replied, 'I never knew you."[31] Notice how the demon actually drives the man to repentance by his temptation rather than to damnation. C.S. Lewis seems to explore a very similar preoccupation of the demons in his *The Screwtape Letters*.

---

30. Nicolson, 351.

31. Siegfried Wenzel, trans., *Preaching in the Age of Chaucer: Selected Sermons in Translation* (Washington, D.C.: Catholic University of America Press, 2008), 28.

21. How might we account for Chaucer's bawdiness in many of his tales?

> Many critics treat the bawdiness as an integral part to Chaucer's display a vast array of characters motivated by a range of desires—some good, many selfish and crude. The Summoner will tell a particular kind of hostile tale including an embarrassing amount of farting because he is the summoner, and everything we have been told about him suggests that he is just the sort of fellow who will stoop to fart jokes to mock the Friar. It is the same for the Miller and the Reeve. While this is primarily a commentary on the kinds of folks professing to go on pilgrimage, most of whom have imaginations filled with anything but confession and repentance, Chaucer must find the bathroom humor and the endless bed tricks quite funny or at least wryly amusing at some level. He is, after all, the actual author of the tales he tells. We have such scant biographical material of Chaucer's own life, particularly any direct commentary on his work, that it is difficult to navigate by Chaucer's moral compass, but we would do well to consider the claims Chaucer makes about the source and character of *true* gentility (not merely hereditary gentility) in the following poem. (It will also give you a chance to try to read some Middle English.)

> *Gentilesse: Moral Balade of Chaucer*

> THE FIRSTE stok, fader of gentilesse—

What man that claymeth gentil for to be,
Must folowe his trace, and alle his wittes dresse
Vertu to sewe, and vyces for to flee.
For unto vertu longeth dignitee,
And noght the revers, saufly dar I deme,
Al were he mytre, croune, or diademe.

This firste stok was ful of rightwisnesse,
Trewe of his word, sobre, pitous, and free,
Clene of his goste, and loved besinesse,
Ageinst the vyce of slouthe, in honestee;
And, but his heir love vertu, as dide he,
He is noght gentil, thogh he riche seme,
Al were he mytre, croune, or diademe.

 Vyce may wel be heir to old richesse;
But ther may no man, as men may wel see,
Bequethe his heir his vertuous noblesse;
That is appropred unto no degree,
But to the firste fader in magestee,
That maketh him his heir, that can him queme,
Al were he mytre, croune, or diademe.

FURTHER DISCUSSION
AND REVIEW

Master what you have read by reviewing and integrating the different elements of this classic.

SETTING AND CHARACTERS
Be able to compare and contrast the personalities (including strengths, weaknesses, and mannerisms) of each character. How does the setting affect the characters?

PLOT
Be able to describe the beginning, middle, and end of each story told, along with specific details that move the plots forward and make them compelling (or not). This includes the success or downfall (or both) of each character as well as each narrator's place in the broader frame tale.

CONFLICT

Go through the narrator list and describe the tension between any and all main narrators. Then, think about whether any of the characters in the stories have internal conflict (in their own minds). Is there any overt conflict (fighting), or conflict with impersonal forces?

THEME STATEMENTS

Be able to describe what this classic is telling us about the world. Is the message true? What truth can we take from the plot, characters, conflict, and themes (even if the author didn't believe that truth)? Do any objects take on added meaning because of repetition or their place in the story (i.e., do any objects become symbols)? Be able to interact with and give examples for the following theme statements:

- Nobility and knavery are found in men from all walks of life; neither the rich, nor the poor, neither the sacred, nor the secular, the well-born, nor low-born are immune to sin and corruption.
- A church in which priests and friars are rich and gluttonous and take payments for their services is a church badly in need of reform.
- Stories are told by people with biases and prejudices; we should always be ready to listen to what they say with a grain of salt, especially if

they have a motive for telling the story to make somebody look bad.

Finally, compose your own theme statement about some element, large or small, of this classic. Then, use the Bible and common sense to assess the truth of that theme statement. Identify your own key words or borrow from the following list as a starting point: *quitting; the three estates; corruption; pilgrimage; story-telling; levels of narration; sources and retellings; crudity.*

A NOTE FROM THE PUBLISHER:
TAKING THE CLASSICS QUIZ

Once you have finished the worldview guide, you can prepare for the end-of-book test. Each test will consist of a short-answer section on the book itself and the author, a short-answer section on plot and the narrative, and a long-answer essay section on worldview, conflict, and themes.

Each quiz, along with other helps, can be downloaded for free at www.canonpress.com/ClassicsQuizzes. If you have any questions about the quiz or its answers or the Worldview Guides in general, you can contact Canon Press at service@canonpress.com or 208.892.8074.

Elizabeth Howard is an adjunct faculty member at Bethlehem College & Seminary and is pursuing her PhD in English at the University of Minnesota. She has taught a range of literature, rhetoric, composition, and language courses at The Potter's School and Mars Hill Academy. She and her husband Zach, who also teaches at Bethlehem, have two daughters.